A-POC

A-POC MAKING

ISSEY MIYAKE
& DAI FUJIWARA

Contents

10   Catalogue | Katalog

60   Subtitles

65   A-POC MAKING at the Vitra Design Museum Berlin
       Mateo Kries

68   Clothing for the Future – Captured by Imagination and Technology
       Issey Miyake

70   A-POC, A-POS, A-POM & A-POE
       Dai Fujiwara

74   Biographies

81   A-POC 1997 – 2001

102   German version | Deutsche Texte

110   Acknowledgements | Danksagung

110   Picture Credits | Bildnachweis

111   Imprint | Impressum

I have endeavored to experiment to make fundamental changes to the system of making clothes. Think: a thread goes into a machine that in turn, generates

complete clothing using the latest computer technology and eliminates the usual needs for cutting and sewing the fabric.

Issey Miyake

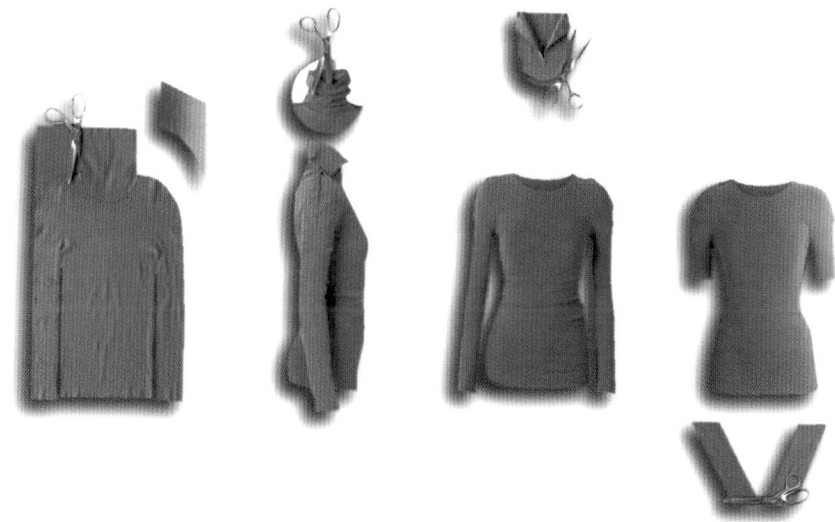

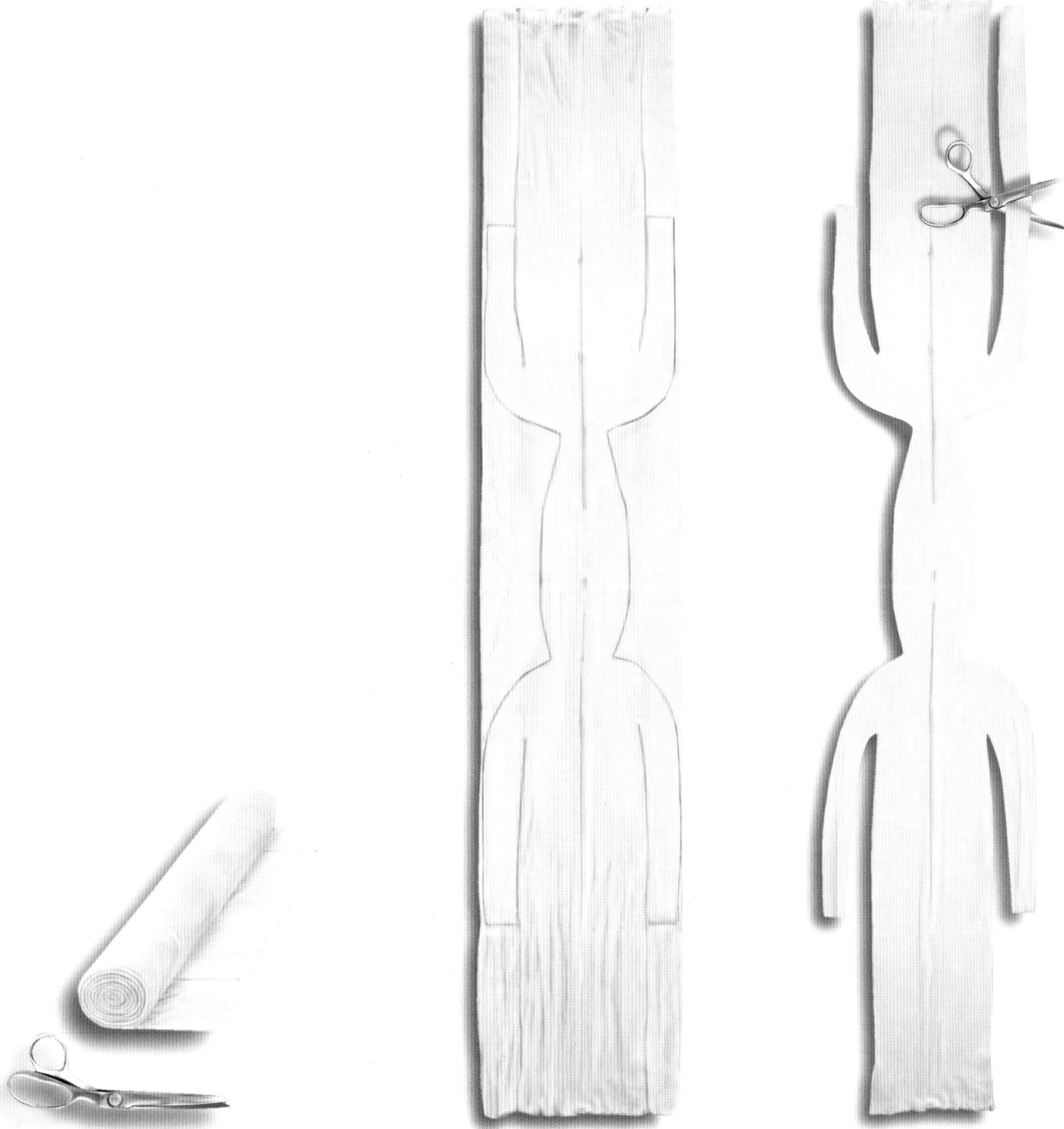

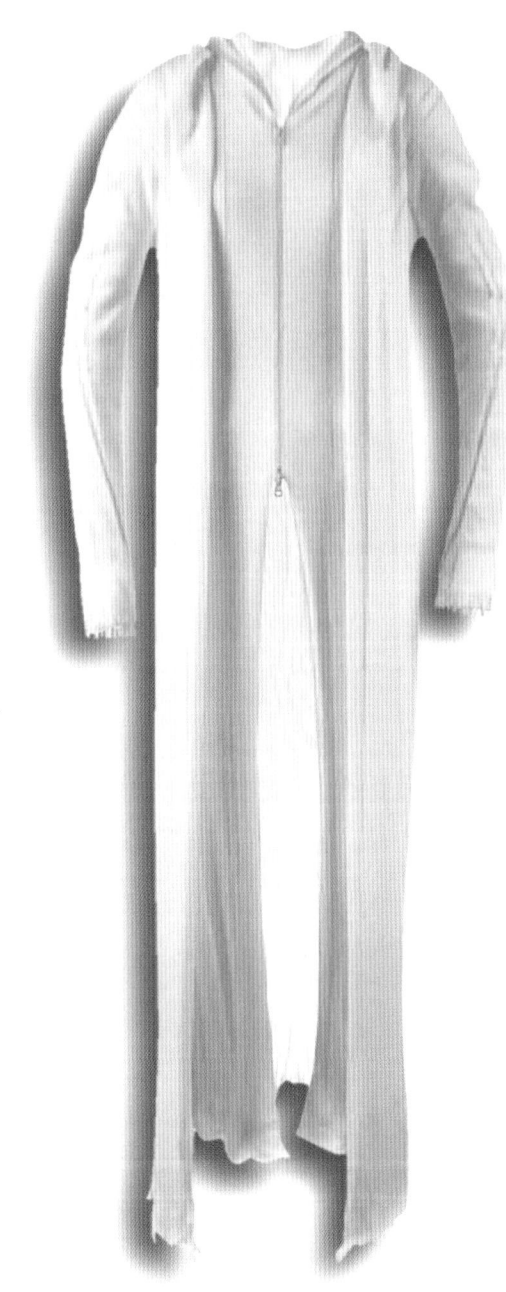

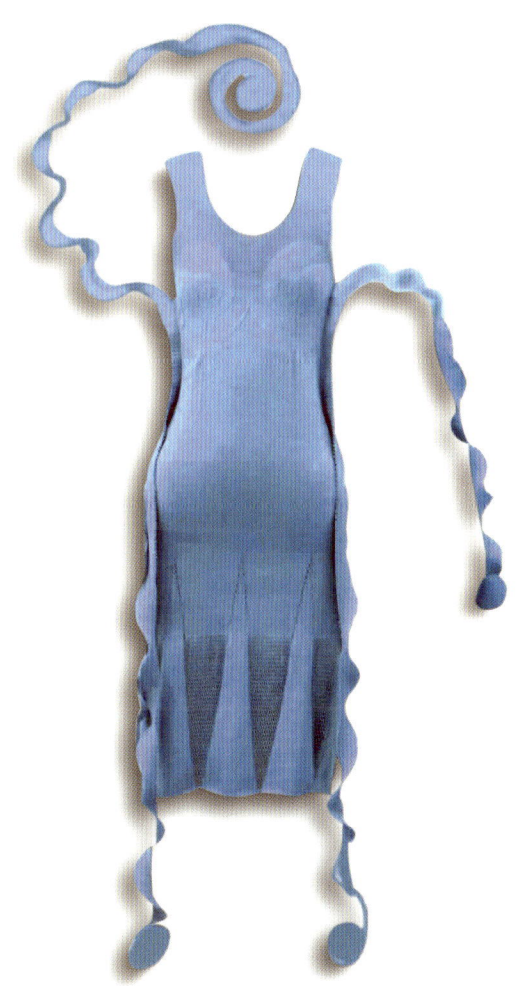

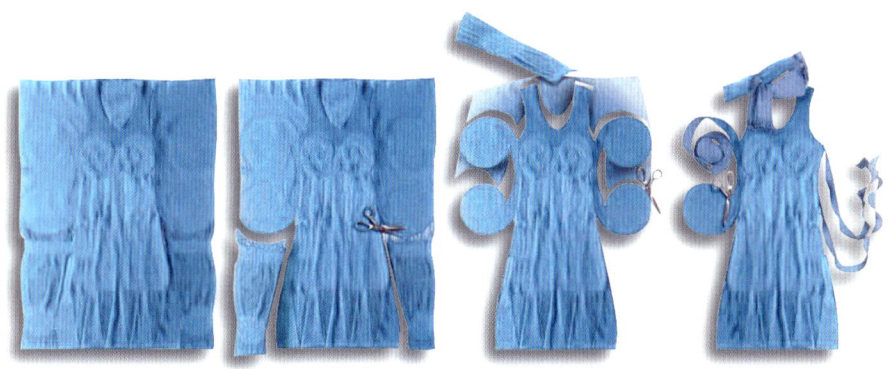

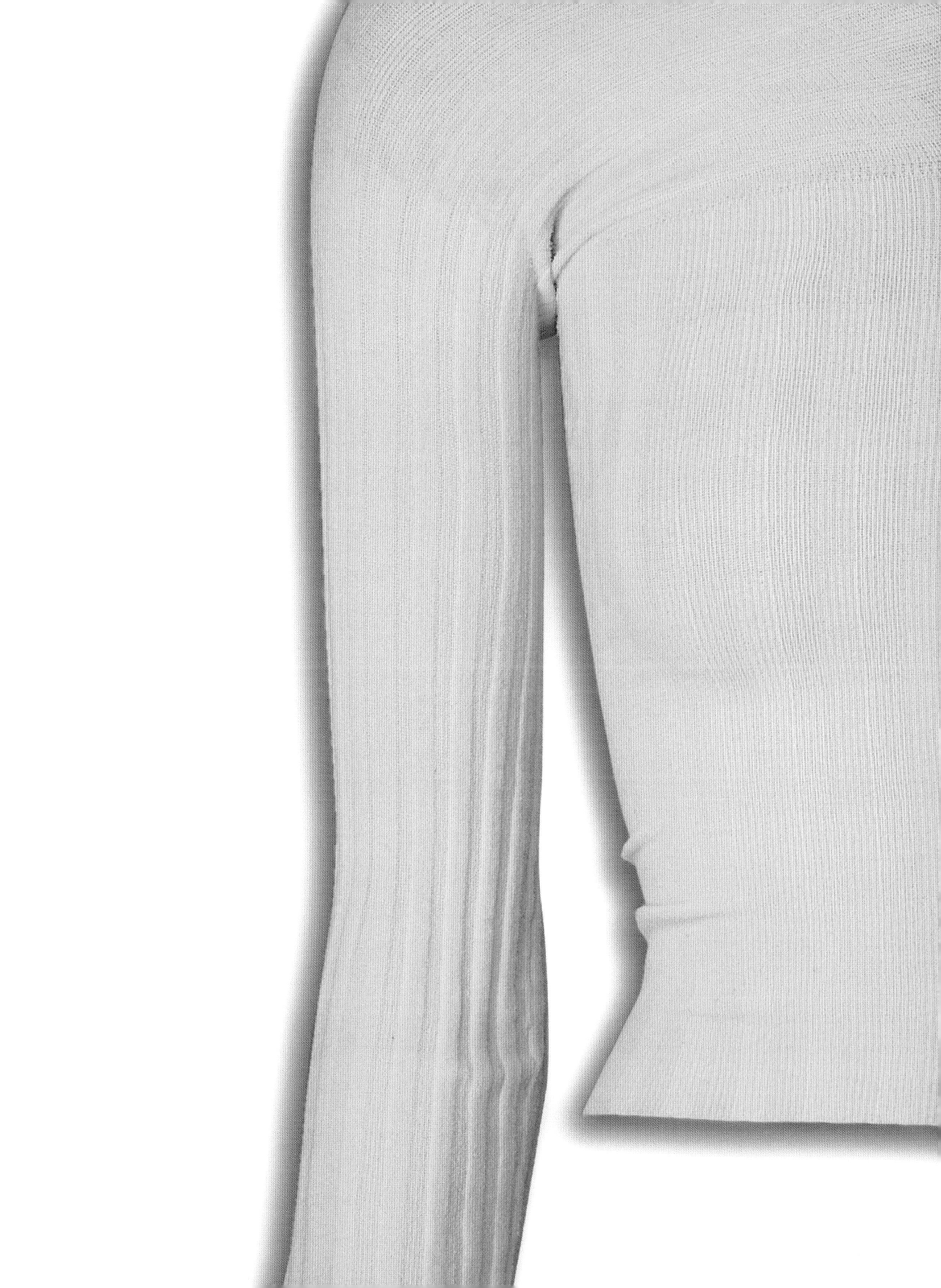

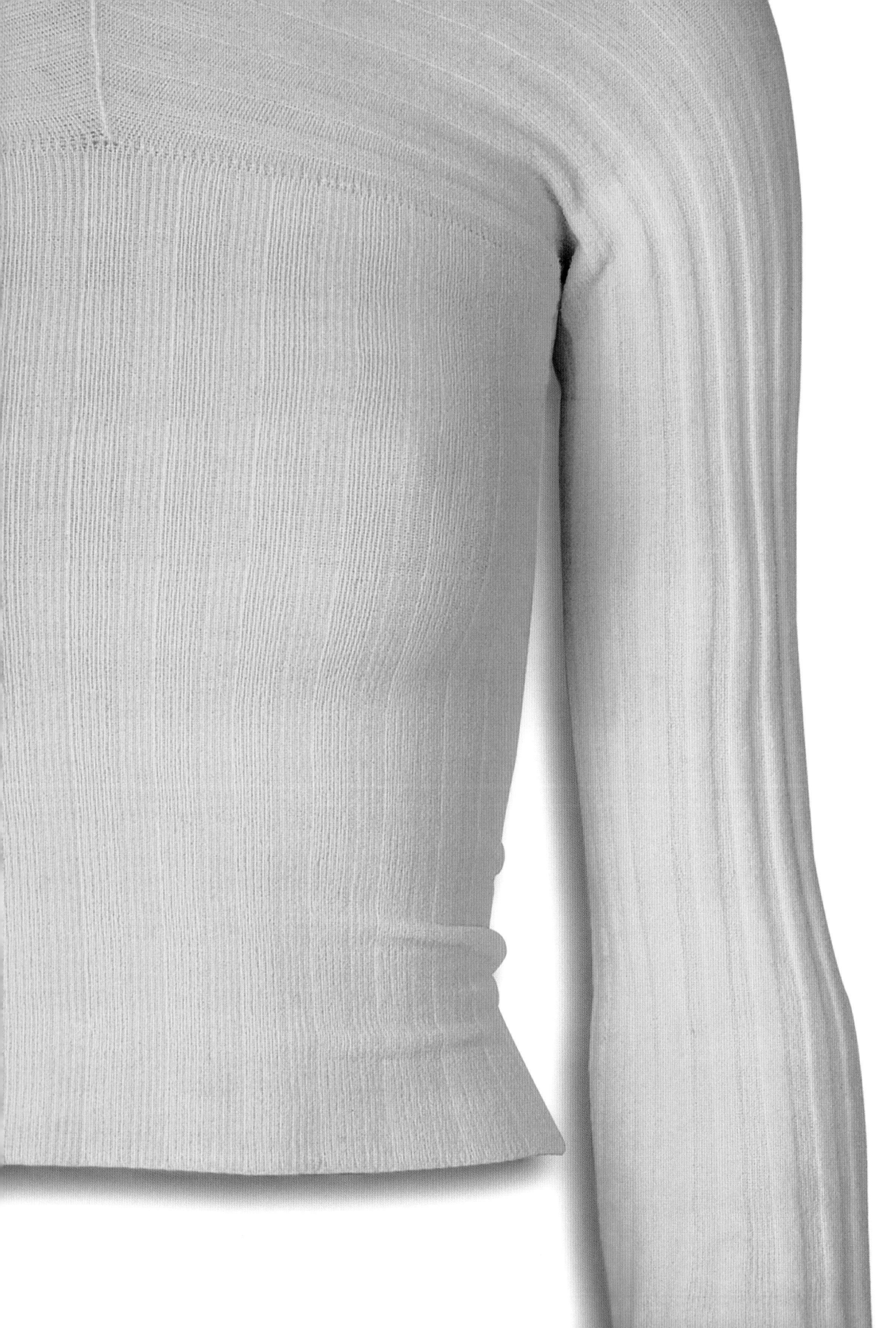

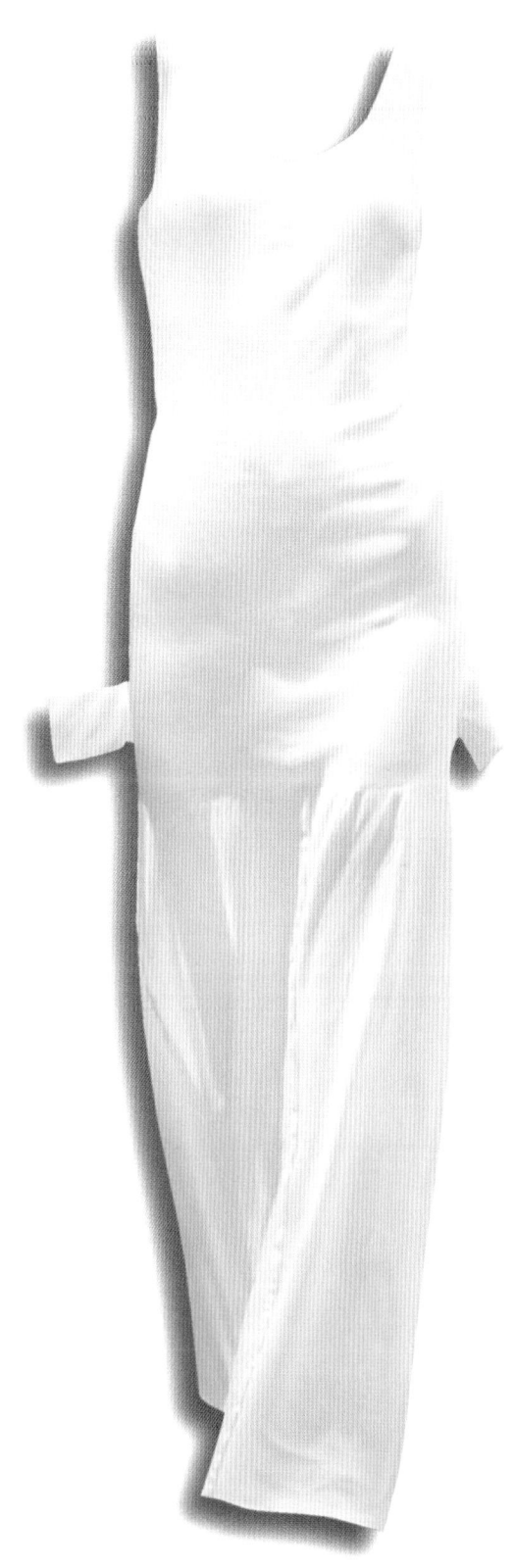

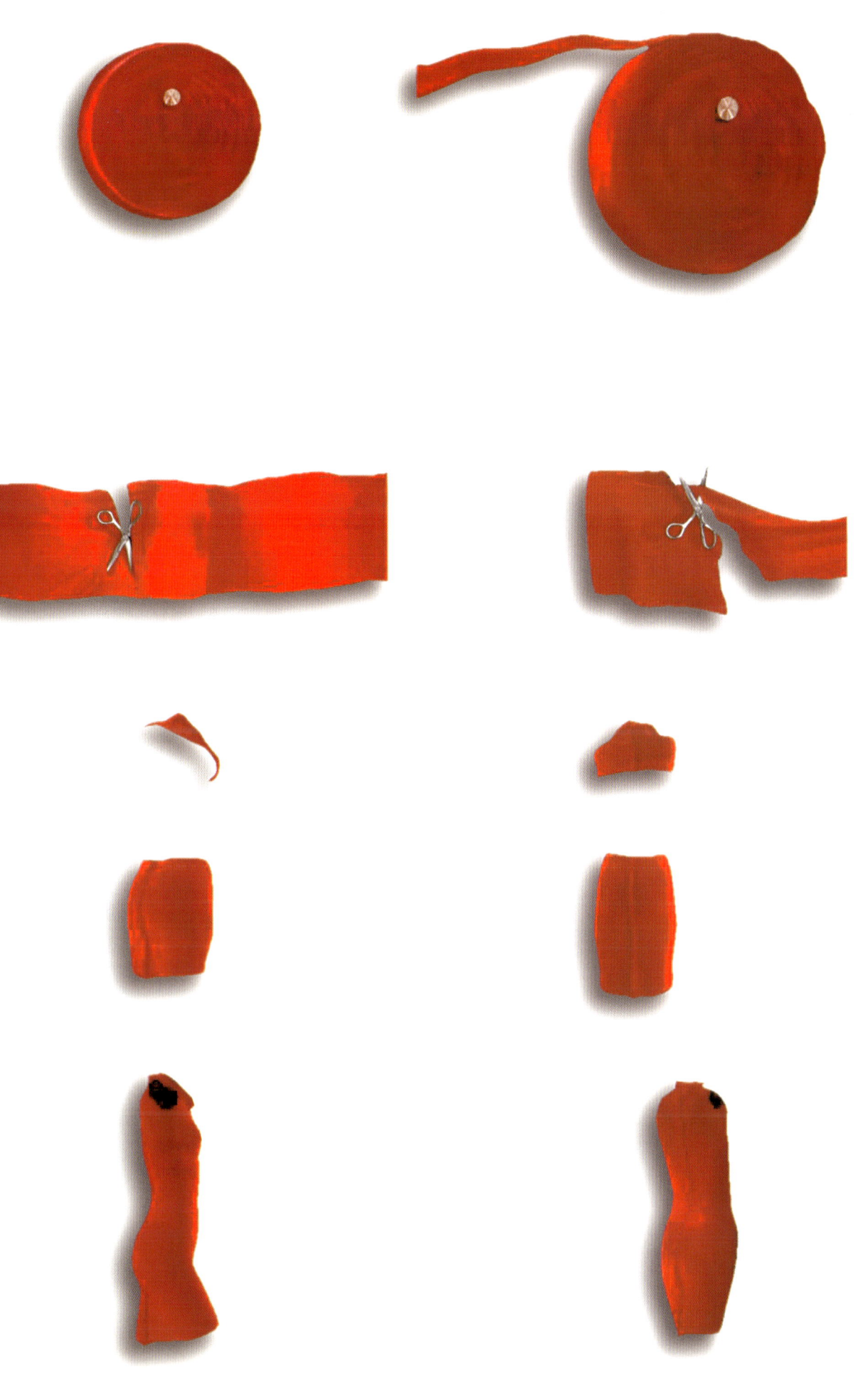

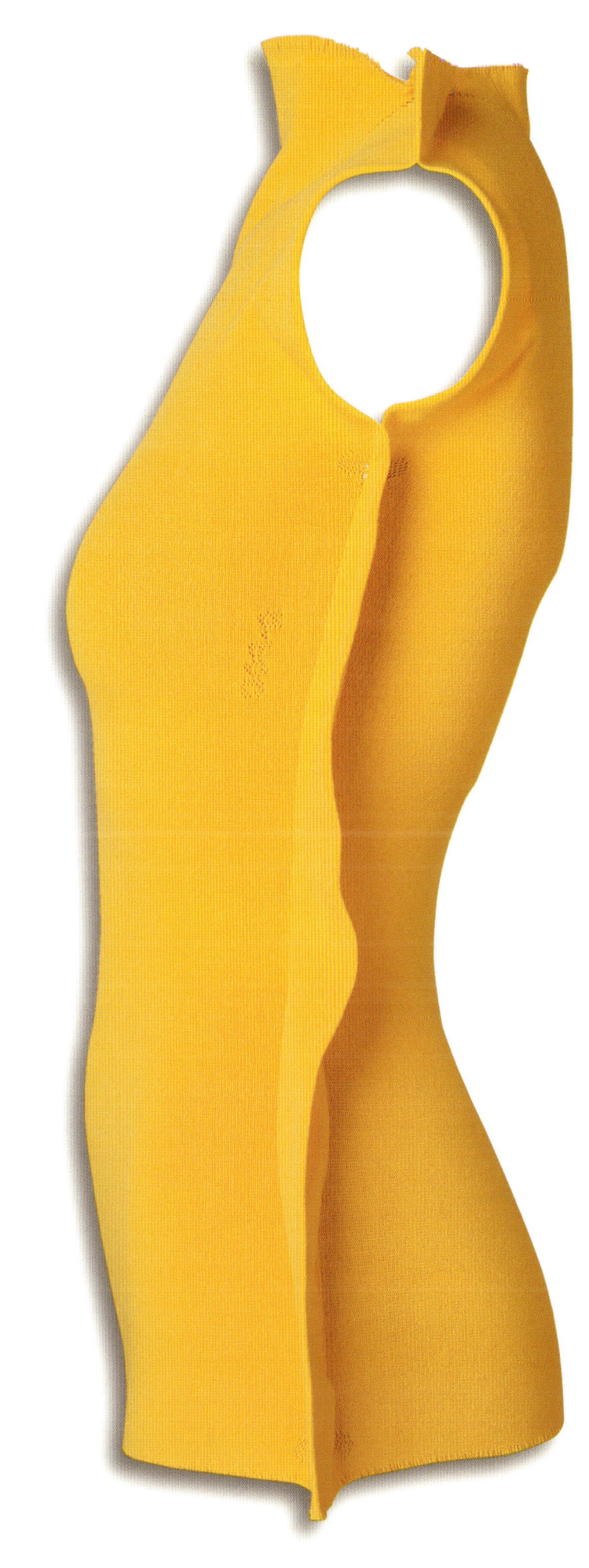

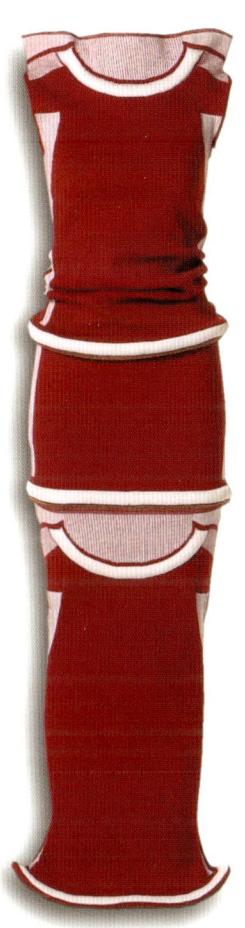

  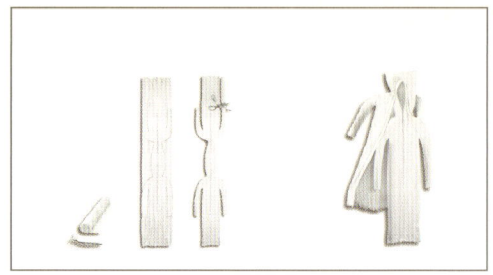
  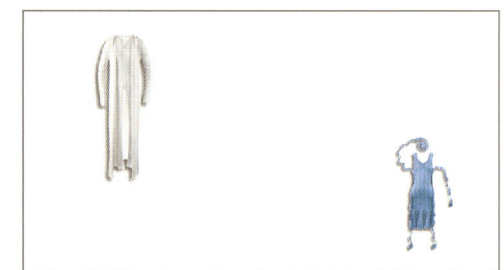

Baguette

Spring–Summer 2000 +

Like the French loaf of bread after which it is named, "Baguette" is a group of stretch knits that can be cut at any place: the fabric will not unravel even if it is cut where there are no lines of demarcation. The cotton/nylon stretch material is comfortable throughout the year. Available in plain or floral knits, with tapes cut along the seams, or in panelled packaging.

Baguette

Spring–Summer 2000 +

Frame Work: Woven

Autumn–Winter 2001+

A group of seven dress designs produced with the same "frame" but using different warp and weft yarns. This is the beauty of the "frame" product design concept. Geometric patterns; colourful horizontal stripes; a transparent and shiny motif, or gathered pieces in stretch wool. The basic "Frame Work" is a template that enables the creation of up to 64 varieties in one entire range. The production of one small lot accommodates a wide range of individual demands.

Frame Work: Woven

Autumn–Winter 2001+

Alien

Autumn–Winter 1999

"Alien" is an advanced version of "King" & "Queen". It is made from a folded tube of airy mesh knit which creates additional layers. Characteristic of A-POC, this is a means of creating clothes that invites the wearer to participate in the creation of the final design.

One Piece

Spring–Summer 2001

The group consists of six knit dresses with different expressions, created from one pattern. The tank tops are the same, but the bottoms are in different mesh knit patterns. Three skirt lengths are available. The variations are endless; the spiral tapes and the mesh scarf cut at the seams can be tied or untied for different effects.

+: the idea of this model is further developed in following collections

60

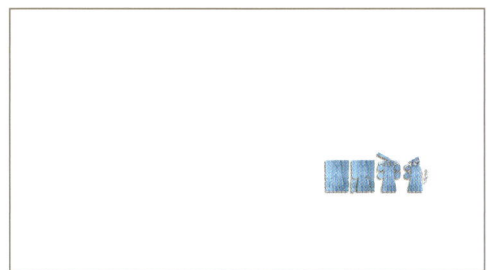  
  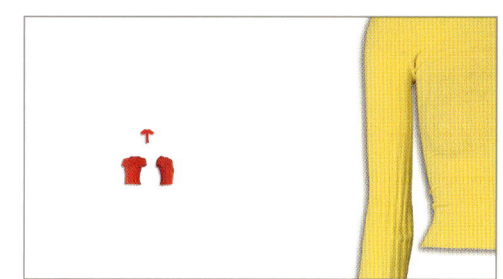

One Piece
Spring–Summer 2001

Zoo
Autumn–Winter 2001

A group of knits that resembles whimsical animals found nowhere else in the world. They come in the same shape but in different colours, like animal crackers. The group includes "Turtle", which can be worn with arms and legs emerging from any of the vertical, horizontal or middle openings; "Octopus", with quirky movements; "Monkey", with a jungle tree branch; "Teddy Bear" with sections stuffed with cotton wool, and the jolly "Panther".

Zoo: Monkey
Autumn–Winter 2001

King & Queen
Spring–Summer 1999

Like a magic carpet, when the roll is unfurled an entire wardrobe is revealed (dress, shirt, skirt, hat, socks and bag), to be cut out with a pair of scissors along the lines of demarcation. "King" and "Queen" are composed of active, positive and energetic designs. On another note, A-POC is environmentally friendly, as it greatly reduces fabric waste.

Queen
Spring–Summer 1999

Spider
Spring–Summer 2000 +

Teeny sweater which, when stretched, becomes a small, medium or even a large size. After wearing, a simple tug at either end of the sweater returns it to its original tiny form. Made from a stretch wool yarn with amazing elasticity, like a spider's web, which fits lightly to the body. It comes in solid, bright colours or multi-coloured stripes. A thick grey and brown yarn knit has also recently been added.

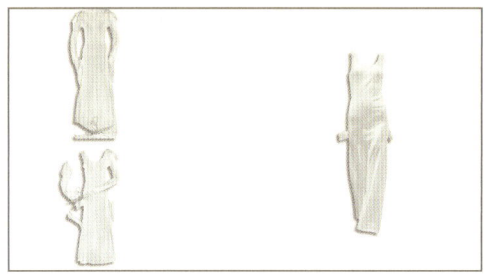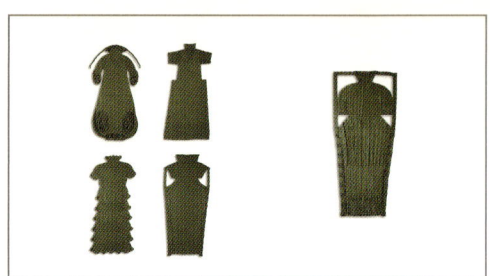
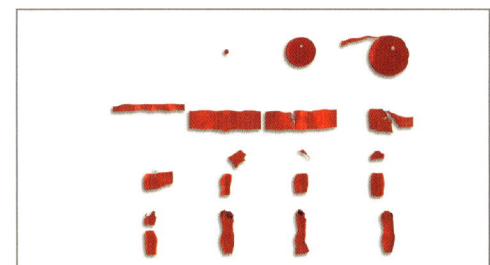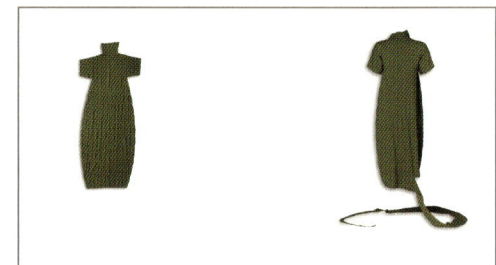

Spider
Spring–Summer 2000 +

Just Before
Spring–Summer 1998
An industrial knitting machine is computer-programmed to produce a continuous series of tube-knit dresses from one strand of thread. Undoubtedly one of the most innovative clothes-making techniques, this transforms the very system of fashion from its conception to its realization, a total departure from the traditional method of clothes-making which is to cut the fabric and then sew it to form a shape. Each piece, just before becoming a dress, may be cut out in a variety of different ways. This enables every woman to participate in the last stage of the creation of her own dress, using her own criteria. "Just Before" set the stage for the birth of A-POC.

Just Before
Spring–Summer 1998

Le Feu
Spring–Summer 1999
The stretch nylon knit is called "Le Feu", flame, because its knitted pattern resembles the sun rising. A skirt and T-shirt are in corporated into a series of square panels; unexpected shapes are created when these are worn, as the sleeve direction changes or the neckline expands.

Berlin Homage
Autumn–Winter 2001
The city of Berlin, the symbol of the unification of East and West, is one of the most exciting metropolises in the world today, with many striking buildings being constructed. "Berlin Homage" is a group of six different dresses resembling high-rise buildings. They each look unique, so it is hard to believe that they are merely variations on a single shape and knit pattern.

Berlin Homage
Autumn–Winter 2001

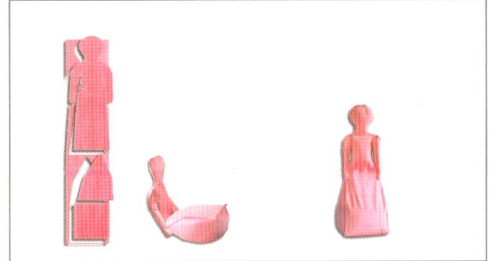  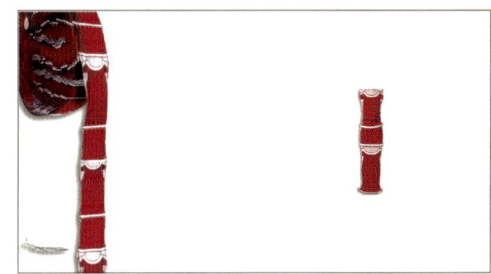

Baguette
Spring–Summer 2000

Mobile
Autumn–Winter 2000 +

This is a mobile interior-object. The chair and pillows have some of the functions of humans and some of clothes. The human-shaped "Midas" can be used as a sofa for sitting, a bed for lying down or a doll to hold. The lightweight chair can be moved around easily. The pillow "Pao Pao" can also be used as a jacket or trousers, and one sweater has a pillow at the end of its sleeve. With your own imagination you can expand the range of uses. "Mobile" is the best piece to relax with, playfully or peacefully.

Caravan
Autumn–Winter 2000

Inspired by the image of a desert caravan. It includes three items: a slightly wild coat with a hood, a coat with a collar, and a skirt. "Caravan" is thickly woven with cotton vertical threads and thick and thin wool horizontal threads. By incorporating the body width, a three-dimensional shape has been added to the previously flat A-POC.

Caravan
Autumn–Winter 2000

Pain de Mie
Spring–Summer 2000 +

Like the rectangular loaf of bread after which it is named, "Pain de Mie" is woven in a rectangular shape so that you can select the length and shape of the collar and sleeve. It is produced entirely by weaving, without using any needles for sewing. Cool, pastel-coloured cotton in a simple weave gives it a gentle and natural flavour. Strings, cut out at the seams, are used as ties to adjust fit.

Eskimo
Autumn–Winter 1999

"Eskimo" was shown to introduce a mystery of the A-POC adventure. Graphic patterns, in black or ice-grey, are padded with cotton to make raised, two-tone reliefs. The shapes – comfortable shirts with skirts or trousers – are made with a light but warm knit.

final double-page:
Eskimo
Autumn–Winter 1999

Issey Miyake and Dai Fujiwara at the Vitra Design Museum Berlin

Mateo Kries

Issey Miyake is seen as one of the leading clothing designers of our time. His career has taken him from Japan to Paris, London, New York and back to Tokyo. Long before fashion began to take inspiration from popular culture, Miyake was searching for ways to interpret clothing as something other than elite haute couture. Miyake's work is a fusion of Japanese and western influences, which proves what wonderful results can arise from global thinking and acting. "Making things" – this simple credo characterizes the natural way in which Issey Miyake works. It became the title for an exhibition, which was opened in 1998 at the Fondation Cartier pour l'art contemporain in Paris and showed the impressive results of Issey Miyake's work.

Miyake looks for real challenges and solutions. One of these challenges is found in the relationship between body and clothing, which he has interpreted in many new ways. Miyake succeeds in almost offhandedly creating designs of an unpretentious beauty, which seem to come from another world beyond trends and fashions. Now Miyake has found a new challenge in the same vein: the process of producing clothing. He started working on this challenge with Dai Fujiwara, one of the many talents emerging from Miyake's design studio in Tokyo in recent years. Together they have completely rethought the complex manufacturing process of making clothes – from the generation of raw materials through to the machines used and the delivery system, all the way to the fitting of the wearer. The result is A-POC (A Piece of Cloth). Miyake and Fujiwara opened A-POC spaces in Paris and Tokyo in 2000, and now A-POC is presented for the first time outside these two cities in this book and the accompanying exhibition.

When Issey Miyake and Dai Fujiwara visited the Vitra Design Museum Berlin in October 2000, our new museum in Berlin was only four months young. Miyake and Fujiwara talked enthusiastically about their new concept and rolled out a number of different fabrics from their A-POC collection, whose patterns and fretwork at first glance reminded us of kilims. On closer inspection we recognized that in these rolls of fabric were hidden complete clothing ensembles, including a wallet, a bag and a hat, waiting to be cut out! The obvious beauty of this creation fascinated us as much as the strength of the A-POC concept itself. In its radical ground-laying work, the idea of A-POC corresponds to a design ideal which is also the premise of the work of our museum: that successful design has to recreate its foundations constantly from the knowledge of its own predecessors and can only obtain its aesthetic power from this. A-POC is proof of the validity of this thesis. The decision to concentrate on A-POC in an exhibition and a publication was followed by an inspiring and productive collaboration, whose results are to be seen here and for which we heartly thank all participants. For the Vitra Design Museum Berlin, this exhibition is not only the first exclusively created for our new museum, but also a challenge for our future work.

A-POC is based on the possibility of producing endless lengths of new fabric with previously unknown properties with the help of computer-programmed machines. Patterns can be worked into the textile, and a sophisticated system of links and holes between the two sides of the tube allows the user to cut out seamless clothing from the fabric in different variations. The computer can be used to define characteristics at different points of the fabric, and some of the fabrics can be cut at any point. With these and other possibilities, A-POC has been able to free itself from the limitations of conventional tailoring, which were previously dictated by the properties of fabric, pattern and sewing technique. Instead of the strict matrix of warp and weft that must be sewn in the shape of the human body, a seamless continuum emerges which comes closer to the human form than ever before.

A-POC allows an ambition to become reality that has been a leading motif in the history of design: to create an object out of a single piece. Put the raw material into a machine, and take out the finished product at the other end! This dream is much more than just a simple belief in technology. Since the Industrial Revolution began, it has been stood for optimum resource utilization, rationalization of the manufacturing process and machine aesthetics. These are reflected in Miyake's work as the effort to start with a single piece of cloth in creating a design. With A-POC, Miyake and Fujiwara reach a new dimension in this effort. Thanks to computer technology, another raw material is incorporated into the production process more closely than ever: human creativity. The machine becomes a flexible system, which reacts directly to the instructions of the creator. Similar to the computer-to-plate printing process or to machines that mill out a three-dimensional model based only on computer drawings, a complicated process becomes a small step that can be influenced at any time. On the user side as well, Issey Miyake and Dai Fujiwara achieve unforeseen creative freedom by assigning A-POC an element of interactivity, which lets the user create his or her own piece of clothing. The result is an ingeniously simple process. What two designers have started and reproduced by machine can then be shaped into any form by the user, according to his or her own wishes and needs.

Using the basic idea of A-POC, Issey Miyake and Dai Fujiwara have developed a multitude of models and variations, which are introduced in this book. Their aesthetics are characterized by equal contributions from all participants: the designers, the technology and the user. As a result of true innovation, these aesthetics have an inner logic and are much more than fashionable. They are comparable to the aesthetics of furniture design of the 1920s, when tubular steel revolutionized production and design processes. In a similar sense, A-POC points to the future and shows that the integration of technology into the design process can have a clarifying influence, in that it allows an object to be reduced to its essence. Issey Miyake and Dai Fujiwara are using technology for a formal limitation and, at the same time, this technology is giving a freedom never before known to both designers and users.

This book presents the A-POC items as if they were anatomical specimens. Clothing becomes science; it is dissected and redefined from its beginnings. The exhibition A-POC MAKING and this book are a glimpse into the laboratory of Issey Miyake and Dai Fujiwara. Although they do not clone or perform feats of magic, they are working on a holistic image of the human being and its clothing which could make history. It combines the individual wishes of the user with the demands of an economical production process, computer technology with economical use of resources, a unique artistic document with portable clothing that can accompany us every day. And, finally, it once again places in the spotlight the person for whom the clothes are made. At the moment you release your own piece of cloth from the A-POC textile, you feel that you yourself are the clothing designer – or, as two of the first A-POC models are named, a "king" or "queen".

Clothing for the Future
Captured by Imagination and Technology

Issey Miyake

After handing over the design of the Issey Miyake label to my protegé in the year 2000, I took off on an adventure. The voyage we have undertaken is to a planet we have named A-POC. My companions and partners on this journey are Dai Fujiwara and several other young people. I am confident that, with their imagination and lack of preconceptions, they will work with me to find "a state of clothing that reflects its time and lifestyle" – something for which I am always searching.

The latter half of the eighteenth century saw the Industrial Revolution, spurred on greatly by the inventions of the spinning machine and the steam engine. This in turn gave birth to a new middle class, particularly after the French Revolution. These social and industrial upheavals changed the history of clothing and popularized fashion, which had hitherto been only for the privileged aristocracy. From these beginnings eventually came haute couture, with a host of new creative ideas; in time, prêt-à-porter (ready-to-wear) was derived from that. Fashion, ever since, has been diversifying as the world around it changes.

Once again our society is poised to make dramatic changes based upon developments in science and technology. Will fashion be able to afford to keep the same old methodology? I have endeavoured to experiment to make fundamental changes to the system of making clothes. Think: a thread goes into a machine that, in turn, generates completed clothing using the latest computer technology, eliminating the usual needs for cutting and sewing the fabric. The idea stemmed from my desire to make a contribution to environmental protection and the conservation of resources. The process not only cuts down on resources and labour, but is also a means to recycle thread. I first introduced this idea, calling it "Just Before" in my Spring/Summer 1998 Collection. Different dress shapes were knitted in a continuous tube and the final step in their completion was made by the wearer. By the Spring/Summer 2000 Collection the project had been named A-POC, which stands for A Piece Of Cloth and continues to evolve. Recent versions have been "Woven", an integrated formulation of textiles; "Mobile", spreading widely; "Angel", children's clothing; and "Framework", the variation of specific frames. We are still in a phase of creating formulas for industrial products, but the possibilities are infinite. With a little imagination, we might even be able to go beyond making clothes to making robots! I believe that technology can function only as long as we have the ability to imagine, a sense of curiosity and a love for our fellow men.

The A-POC concept was born in Japan, and presented in Paris where originality is cherished. A-POC will now take its first steps in Berlin, a city that symbolizes the unification of the East and the West. With each visit to Berlin, I become more and more fascinated by its willingness to contribute to international society, its capacity to appreciate diverse cultures and the dynamic energy of its reconstruction. It is interesting that the Bauhaus tradition, the integration of art and technology, was born in Germany. The Vitra Design Museum might be called the successor to the Bauhaus movement, inextricably linked to everyday living. The museum owns an extensive collection of contemporary furniture and related materials, and is one of the first to focus on industrial design: the integration of art and technology. The Museum fully understands our ambition to explore future design for the twenty-first century through its most intimate form: clothing design for human beings.

I would like to express my heartfelt gratitude to the Vitra Design Museum Berlin for the opportunity to exhibit our work. It will bring me the utmost delight if the people of Berlin enjoy the exhibition.

A-POC, A-POS, A-POM & A-POE

Dai Fujiwara

A-POC is an acronym coined from "A Piece of Cloth" and is a play on the word "Epoch". "A Piece of Cloth" is a constantly evolving concept that will translate into different forms from this epoch to the next. These are all connected by an invisible thread both to the ancient days of their origin, as well as to the present metamorphosis, i.e. A-POC. The process of making things advances but never severs its ties with the knowledge of the age that preceded it.

A Piece of Cloth can be traced to and found in ancient myths. Picture a painting: the Piece of Cloth softly draped over the shoulders of a voluptuous heavenly maiden, drawn with clear but gentle colours, is an A-POC. The cloth in the picture is dancing, lightly floating in the air, transparently thin, hinting at its technological expertise. It is an ancient time. A man must have created the painting, so I guess A Piece of Cloth existed even then. But then it must have done, for it was A-POC that always inspired hope, courage and dreams in one's life.

In this spirit, we are calling our thread A-POS (A Piece of String). It is still unknown how much influence will come from the innovative materials to be born from this latest nano- and biotechnology, but its origins were hinted at in materials found with buried ancient artefacts. An unbelievably tenacious material, which created textiles using a revolutionary spinning technique, was a thin piece of string, based on the spirit of making things. The Piece of String could be so feather-light that it might melt if exposed to the light of the sun's rays.

When an excavated thread from a particular era is chemically analysed, sometimes molecules of sericin and fibroin are detected – in this manner, we can identify it as silk. According to documents, the silk fibre found in the Maotai (Changsha Mawangadui) tomb was thinner than our present fibres. Silk fibre is made of polymers, meaning that it takes on a slender form. The longer the fibres, the faster the spinning speed can be; and, ultimately, the production costs can be reduced.[1] The cloth in the painting might actually have been floating. I can imagine the faces of the ancient engineers: men who invented a way of spinning without the thin threads becoming tangled; who designed looms that would not make faults; and who pondered the question of whether it was best to deliver the finished cloth rolled or folded.

There is really little difference between ancient times and today in terms of the efforts and imagination required to move forward in terms of technology and production-efficiency. The history of silk is filled with innovations. There is a vast quantity of data available, from the sericulture of China to the proofs of Mendel's Law experimented with silkworms in the beginning of the Twentieth Century in Japan. There is a series of astonishing innovations: the development of silkworm-feed, thread-making technologies, genetic hybridization, and even cloning.[2] The power of imagination has fuelled A Piece of Cloth throughout history. This force could be called "A Power of Creation".

Given all this, what is left for human beings to invent, and how will these new materials be used? Perhaps a hybrid from a silkworm and a spider, or polyester extracted from a rice plant? The concept of "nature" and what is natural may inevitably change. It is exciting to think what these innovations might mean for A-POC. Innovation empowers human beings and, as a natural result, A-POC.

Let us now think of machines. In the world of A-POC, we call our machine A-POM (A Piece of Machine). When making cloth, the fundamental principle moving A-POM is the one-and-zero binary-language principle. People in the field of engineering, when given this description, would respond, "That is a computer." Please refer to the simple diagram on the next page. It looks like a chess-board. But when the diagram is transmitted to the machine, the thread moves up and down and weaves or knits the cloth. The same movement applies to weaving or knitting. White is the signal for "sink", and black the signal for "surface"; the machine interprets the diagram, knowing from it whether to weave a piece of fabric that might dance in the air, or to knit a T-shirt. "Language" can be communicated: we can program black to be "forward" and white to be "backward"; we can even make up a simple game. There is a digital language in the process of making textiles. Analysing A-POC clothing, one finds a set of dots. If one is to consider these dots to be like genes in a human body, each A-POC dress may consist of as many as 200 million "genes". And once the digital pattern of the dress is established, as many as needed can be commercially "cloned". And these genes or the threads "crossing points" are where flows could occur. It takes courageous factory staff to produce A-POC, using technology and their imagination to weave without flaws. Today's A-POC may be receiving the benefit of the computer revolution in the most straightforward manner.

Looking at the ancient excavated cloth, one could imagine that the engineers of that time had intuited the basic theory of computer technology. So far as making cloth and the use of thread are concerned, there is no difference between ancient times and the information that is whirring in engineers' heads today. Even if artificial intelligence(AI) were to exist in the near future, it would not bring about any dramatic change in the way A-POC is created. In fact, it might only add to the possible occurrences of natural phenomena.

As long as we have man to spin A-POS, to move A-POM, to make A-POC, we believe that we need A-POE (A Person of Education) to regulate production and business methods. These must address many, including environmental, concerns.

The twentieth century was the "epic epoch" in terms of making things in quantity and diversity with lowered costs, a result of continuous mass production. In prêt-à-porter, which is almost mass-produced haute couture, shapes and colours change every season. This is in opposition to, say, the designs of cars or household appliances, which use a continuous production method for the same product. When the prêt-à-porter season is over, a new one must be created in a flash, so it begins all over again. It is always fresh. In that sense, the global standards of present production systems of the personal computer(PC) or the car may be the beginning of their conversion to something analogous to the prêt-à-porter system. Standardization is required for the reduction of production cost, while a diversification of designs is necessary to meet the wide range of customer demands.[3] Prêt-à-porter was once an innovation, as it reduced production costs while diversifying designs.

"Let us begin," Issey-san says, as he holds a piece of cloth in his hand; let us begin to travel through time and space at a dash; and to transcend all existing value judgements using the force of Imagination as our propellor.

[1] *Xia Nai, The Origin of Chinese Civilization,*
published by Nippon Hoso Kyokai, Tokyo, 1984

[2] *Kametaro Sotoyama, Theory of Silkworm Species,*
published by Maruyamasha Shosekibu, Tokyo, 1909

[3] *The Machine That Changed the World,* edited by Daniel Roos and James P. Womack,
published by R A Rawson Associates Scribner, New York, 1990

Biographies

Issey Miyake

1938	Born in Hiroshima, Japan
1964	Graduated from Tama Art University, Tokyo with a degree in graphic design
1970	Established the Miyake Design Studio (MDS) in Tokyo
1971	Presented collection for the first time overseas, in New York
1973	Joined the French Federation and presented the first Paris collection; it continues to be shown twice a year
1977	Awarded the 1976 Mainichi Design Prize
1978	Published "Issey Miyake East Meets West" (Heibonsha Ltd, Tokyo), a monograph on Miyake's design concept of "One Piece of Cloth"
1983–85	Exhibition "Issey Miyake Specacle: Bodyworks" shown in Tokyo, Los Angeles, San Francisco and London
1986	Started collaboration with Irving Penn, resulting in a series of books and posters Featured as cover story in TIME Magazine (international edition, 27 January)
1988	Exhibition "Issey Miyake A-UN" at Musée des Arts Décoratifs, Paris Started works on pleats
1990	Participated in the exhibition "Energies – 1990" at the Stedelijk Museum, Amsterdam Awarded first Hiroshima Art Prize by the city of Hiroshima Commemorative exhibition of the Hiroshima Art Prize, "Ten Sen Men", at Hiroshima City Museum of Contemporary Art Exhibition "Issey Miyake: Pleats Please" at Touko Museum of Contemporary Art, Tokyo
1991	Designed costumes for Ballet Frankfurt's "The Loss of Small Detail", choreographed by William Forsythe
1992	Exhibition "Issey Miyake '92 Twist" at Naoshima Contemporary Art Museum, Kagawa Received the Asahi Prize

	Designed official uniforms for the Lithuanian athletes at the Barcelona Olympic Games
1993	Launched "Pleats Please Issey Miyake" line
	Decorated as a Chevalier de l'Ordre National de la Légion d'Honneur by the French government
	Received an Honorary Doctorate from the Royal College of Art, London
1997	Exhibition "Isamu Noguchi and Issey Miyake – Arizona" at Marugame Genichiro Inokuma Museum of Contemporary Art, Kagawa
	Received The Medal with Purple Ribbon (Shiju Hosho) for contributions to education and culture from the Japanese government
	Started researches on A-POC
1998	Honored as Person of Cultural Merit by the Japanese government
1998–2000	Exhibition "Issey Miyake Making Things" at Fondation Cartier pour l'art contemporain, Paris; Ace Gallery, New York, and the Museum of Contemporary Art, Tokyo
1999	Published "Irving Penn regards the work of Issey Miyake" (Jonathan Cape, Bullfinch Press, Plume, Schirmer Mosel and Kyuryudo)
	Selected as one of "The most influential Asians of the 20th century" in TIME Magazine (23 August 1999, Asian Issue)
2000	Awarded the Georg Jensen Prize 2000 by Tuborg Foundation, Denmark

Dai Fujiwara

1967   Born in Tokyo, Japan
1995   Graduated from Tama Art University, Tokyo, with a degree in textile design
            Joined the Miyake Design Studio as an assitant in textile design and research
1997   Started researches on A-POC

A-POC 1997 – 2001

1997

Just Before

This was presented in the Issey Miyake Spring–Summer 1998 Collection on 15 October, at l'Ecole des Beaux Arts, Paris. An industrial knitting machine is programmed by a computer to produce a series of tube-knit dresses or shirts continuously connected. Each may be cut out in a variety of ways, enabling each wearer to participate in the customization of her clothes. The name "Just Before" refers to the fact that the knits are created "just before" they are cut out and finished. What was innovative about the concept of "Just Before" was that it marked the development of a totally new and different system from the traditional prêt-à-porter process – from the yarns used up until the time of purchase. The garment is made not by the traditional method of cutting and sewing cloth, but rather by passing yarns through a specially programmed machine with state-of-the-art computer technology. It is also one of the first attempts to allow the wearer to participate in the pleasure and process of clothes-making. This was the starting point for A-POC, which would soon follow.

1998

Tube Knit

This model was presented in the Issey Miyake Autumn–Winter 1998 Collection.

It was made by joining pieces of knitted tubes produced by a computer-programmed industrial knitting machine. The process indicated a new possibility for resource conservation by greatly reducing fabric waste and unnecessary steps in the production process.

Start of the A-POC Project

Issey Miyake, who has constantly aimed to explore the endless possibilities for making clothes that are relevant to any given time and its demands, embarked on the A-POC project to explore its possibilities.

King & Queen ◄

Le Feu ▲

Both models were presented in the Issey Miyake Spring–Summer 1999 Collection. A single piece of cloth was placed on the floor of the entrance hall at l'Ecole des Beaux Arts. Cut by the design staff, the piece of cloth was magically transformed into separate components: a one-piece dress, socks, a hat and a bag. This was the beginning of the presentation. The show received a standing ovation at the "Le Feu" finale, when a procession of mannequins walked down the hall, wearing different permutations of a dress, all linked in a single continuous piece of cloth.

Exhibition "Issey Miyake Making Things" at the Fondation Cartier pour l'art contemporain, Paris ►

An exhibition, focused upon Issey Miyake's activities over the past 10 years, was held at the Fondation Cartier pour l'art contemporain in Paris from 1 October 1998 to 29 February 1999. A-POC drew attention as a suggestion for future of clothing.

1999

Alien ▲ ▶ ▼ ▶
Eskimo

They were among the Issey Miyake Autumn-Winter 1999 Collection held on March 10 at La Grande Halle de la Villette, Salle Charlie Parker, Paris. "Alien" was made of double layers of airy knitted mesh to add interest and depth. "Eskimo", with padded geometric patterns, had three-dimensional interest.

Presentation of A-POC

The first presentation of A-POC as an independent project was held at the Jingumae Studio in Tokyo on 29 March. The show included the A-POC pieces created for the Spring–Summer and Autumn–Winter 1999 Collections.

1999

Performance "Jeux de Tissue" by Yayoi Kusama

At the French Embassy, Tokyo, on 9 April (as part of the "Year of France in Japan") the avant-garde artist Yayoi Kusama created a piece of performance art called "Jeux de Tissue". Using white A-POC "King" and "Queen" as her canvas, Kusama sprayed colourful dots on them and named them "Dots Obsession".

Presentation of the A-POC Spring-Summer 2000 Collection in Paris ▲

Presented at Galerie Ghislaine Hussenot in Paris on 5 October. The remarkable developments of A-POC up to this point were shown: items such as "Millennium Pillow" (which included clothing items as well as accessories and a pillow); "Baguette" (which can be cut at any place); "Pain de Mie" (plain-woven fabrics, not knits); "Feuille" (knits with a flower pattern) and "Spider" (knits with astonishing elasticity).

Exhibition"Issey Miyake Making Things" at the ACE Gallery, New York ◀ ▶

The exhibition had its second venue at the Ace Gallery, New York, from 11 November 1999 to 29 February 2000. Stronger focus was placed upon the displays of A-POC, as compared to the Paris exhibition.

2000

First A-POC space in Aoyama, Tokyo ▲

The A-POC headquarters opened in the Aoyama district of Tokyo on 17 February. The 234 m^2 space contains not only a retail area but also a workspace for design experiments as well as a studio, which can be observed from outside through glass partitions. The interior design was by Tokujin Yoshioka. Combining elements of designing (studio) and of viewing (retail space) into one area is an attempt to actualize the concept that the wearer can participate (by cutting) in the creative process by completing the final stage of design.
Location: 3-17-14 Minami-Aoyama, Minato-Ku, Tokyo

Exhibition "Issey Miyake Making Things" at the Museum of Contemporary Art, Tokyo ▼

The exhibition was shown from 29 April to 20 August. The opening performance was by 100 cheer-leading students wearing uniforms designed by students from the design departments of various schools. The performance conveyed the message of creating through joint effort and of the joy of making things. Over 100,000 visitors attended.

Participation in the "Utsu" exhibition in Stockholm

This exhibition was held at the Museum of Far Eastern Antiquities in Stockholm, Sweden, from 15 May to 18 August, with the concept that the core of Japanese art rests in perception of the invisible. Works of four artists representing contemporary Japanese culture were shown. Issey Miyake exhibited "King" and "Queen" in the colours of the flags of both countries.

2000

Presentation of the A-POC Autumn-Winter 2000 Collection in Paris (next page)

The Collection was presented on 5 June at the Fondation Cartier pour l'art contemporain in Paris. Among the pieces shown were "Dots Obsession" by Yayoi Kusama; "Angel" (for children); "Mobile" (interior pieces actualized through clothing functions); "Fringe" (with unique knitting seams); "Caravan" and "Pollen". Silhouettes, natural textures and varied colours were achieved through the use of woven pieces.

Opening of the A-POC space in Paris ▲

The second A-POC space was opened on 7 September. It was designed by Ronan and Erwan Bouroullec, emerging young French architect brothers. The display areas can be freely created by moving partitions; cutting tables allow the immediate customization of clothes to the clients' wishes.
Location: 47 Rue des Francs-Bourgeois, 75004 Paris

Grand Prize of the Good Design Award 2000 by the Japan Industrial Design Promotion Organization

A-POC received the Grand Prize of the Good Design Award 2000 on 13 October. The selection committee recognized two revolutionary aspects of A-POC. The first was for the introduction of industrial aspects into fashion through applying production processes with less waste, of integrating marketing processes from idea formation all the way to retail sales, and of participation by individual customers. The second is the production-innovation that enables the seemingly contradictory ideas of customization and mass production to exist at the same time.

2001

Presentation of the A-POC Spring-Summer 2001 Collection in Paris

This presentation was held at the Issey Miyake Paris office on 8 February. Among the pieces shown were six "One Piece" dresses (each made from a single piece of yarn and from the same pattern), "Baguette" (with four design selections made by cutting one shirt in different ways) and others.

Performance by Marcus Tomlinson with A-POC "Mobile" for i-D magazine, 2001

Baguette, Frühjahr–Sommer 2000 +
Wie das französische Brot kann «Baguette» an jeder beliebigen Stelle geschnitten werden, weil sein Baumwoll-/Nylongemisch so beschaffen ist, daß es ganz ohne Nähte produziert wird und nicht ausfranst.

Frame Work: Woven, Herbst–Winter 2001 +
Eine Serie von sieben Kleidern, die auf dem selben Prinzip beruhen, aber aus verschieden gewobenen Stoffen bestehen. Aus dem Grundmodell lassen sich bis zu 64 verschiedene Varianten bilden. Mit einer kleinen Serie läßt sich so einer Vielzahl von unterschiedlichen Bedürfnissen nachkommen.

Alien, Herbst–Winter 1999
«Alien» ist eine Weiterentwicklung von den Modellen «King» & «Queen». Mehrere Lagen entstehen, indem die aus lockerem Gewebe bestehende Röhre gefaltet wird. Bei diesem Prozess nimmt der Benutzer an der Herstellung seines Kleidungsstücks teil.

One Piece, Frühjahr–Sommer 2001
Die Serie besteht aus sechs Strickkleidern mit unterschiedlichen Charakteren, die alle aus einem Grundmuster entstehen. Die Oberteile sind die gleichen, aber die Unterteile weisen unterschiedliche Strickmuster auf. Die Variationen sind unendlich; die ausgeschnittenen Spiralbänder und der Schal können mit unterschiedlichen Effekten gebunden werden.

Zoo, Herbst–Winter 2001
Eine Gruppe von Kleidern, die eigenwilligen Tieren ähnelt, wie sie sonst nirgends auf der Welt zu finden sind. Die Gruppe umfaßt «Turtle» («Schildkröte»), bei der Arme und Beine aus jeder der vertikalen, horizontalen oder mittleren Öffnungen herausgeführt werden können; «Octopus», der seltsame Bewegungen vollführt; «Monkey» («Affe»), mit dem Ast eines Dschungelbaums in der Hand; «Teddy Bear», mit gepolsterten Teilen und den fröhlichen «Panther».

King & Queen, Frühjahr–Sommer 1999
Wie auf einem Zauberteppich breitet sich beim Ausbreiten der Rolle eine komplette Kleidungsausstattung aus. Kleid, Hemd, T-Shirt, Mütze, Socken und Tasche werden mit einer Schere entlang der Schnittlinien herausgelöst. Dieses Verfahren reduziert nicht zuletzt den Stoffverschnitt erheblich.

Spider, Frühjahr–Sommer 2000 +
Ein winziges Stück Stoff von erstaunlicher Elastizität, das beim Anziehen zu einem Pullover in der gewünschten Größe wird und anschließend wieder zurückschrumpft. Den kaum fühlbaren Stoff mit den Eigenschaften eines Spinnennetzes gibt es in lebhaften Farben und seit kurzem auch in dickerem grauen und braunen Gewebe.

Just Before, Frühjahr–Sommer 1998
Eine Industriestrickmaschine wird von einem Computer programmiert, um aus einem einzigen Faden einen durchgehenden Schlauch zu stricken, in dem verschiedene Kleider angelegt sind. Dieses innovative Herstellungsverfahren ist eine Neuinterpretation von Mode von ihrer Konzipierung bis zum Endprodukt. Sie bricht mit der traditionellen Methode der Kleiderherstellung, bei der der Stoff geschnitten und anschließend wieder zusammengenäht wird. Jedes Stück kann in einer Viezahl von Variationen ausgeschnitten werden. «Just Before» war die Initialidee für A-POC.

Le Feu, Frühjahr–Sommer 1999
Der Name dieses Modell aus Kunststoff-Stretch spielt auf die aufgehende Sonne an, an die das Strickmuster erinnert. Ein Rock und ein T-Shirt sind in einer Serie von rechteckigen Grundelementen angelegt; unerwartete Formen entstehen beim Tragen, wenn die Richtungen der Arme wechseln oder der Ausschnitt sich ändert. Bei Finale der ersten Präsentation dieses Konzepts waren 23 Models in «Le Feu»-Kleidern durch einen Schlauch verbunden und erhielten standing ovations.

Berlin Homage, Herbst–Winter 2001
Berlin ist das Symbol für die Vereinigung von Ost und West und wird zu einer der aufregendsten Metropolen der Welt, in der zahlreiche beeindruckende Gebäude entstehen. «Berlin Homage» ist eine Serie von sechs verschiedenen Kleidern mit architektonischem Aufbau. Jedes hat einen so eigenständigen Charakter, daß man kaum glaubt, daß alle auf der selben Grundform und dem selben Strickmuster beruhen.

Mobile, Herbst–Winter 2000 +
Bei diesem Modell handelt es sich um ein flexibles Interior-Objekt. Das Sitzmöbel und die Kissen haben teilweise menschliche Eigenschaften, teilweise die von Kleidungsstücken. Das anatomisch geformte «Midas» kann als Sitzmöbel, als Sofa oder als Puppe dienen und ist dank seines geringen Gewichts leicht beweglich. Das Kissen «Pao Pao» beinhaltet auch eine Jacke, eine Hose und einen Pullover mit Kissen an den Enden seiner Ärmel. Mit eigener Kreativität kann der Benutzer weitere Variationen erfinden.

Caravan, Herbst–Winter 2000
Dieses Modell ist inspiriert von einer Wüstenkarawane und umfaßt drei

Elemente: einen ziemlich wilden Kapuzenmantel, einen Mantel mit Kragen und einen Rock. «Caravan» ist dick gewoben aus vertikalen Baumwollfäden und dicken horizontalen Wollfäden. Das entstehende Volumen bringt in die bislang eher auf Zweidimensionalität beruhende A-POC-Serie einen neuen Charakter.

Pain de Mie, Frühjahr–Sommer 2000 +
Wie der kastenförmige Brotlaib, der diesem Modell den Namen gab, ist pain de mie in rechteckiger Form gewoben. Die Länge des Kragens und der Ärmel kann selbst bestimmt werden. Es ist durchgehend gewoben, sodaß jegliche Näharbeit entfällt. Baumwolle in kühlen Pastellfarben gibt diesem Modell einen einfachen, natürlichen Charakter. Streifen, die an den Nähten herausgetrennt werden, dienen zur Fixierung.

Eskimo, Herbst–Winter 1999
«Eskimo» zeigt das Geheimnisvolle an A-POC. Die grafischen Muster, in Schwarz oder Grau, sind mit Baumwolle gefüllt, sodaß Reliefs entstehen. Die Varianten – komfortable Oberteile mit Rock oder Hose – bestehen aus leichtem, aber warmem Stoff.

+: Die Grundidee dieses Modells wird in den folgenden Kollektionen aufgenommen und weiterentwickelt.

Issey Miyake und Dai Fujiwara
im Vitra Design Museum Berlin / Mateo Kries
Issey Miyake gilt als einer der wegweisenden Modeschöpfer unserer Zeit. Sein Werdegang führte von Japan über Paris, London, New York zurück nach Tokio. Lange bevor die Modewelt begann, sich an der populären Kultur zu inspirieren, suchte Miyake nach Ansätzen, Bekleidung anders als elitäre Haute Couture zu interpretieren. Die Synthese aus japanischer und westlichen Kultur, die Issey Miyakes Schaffen durchzieht, beweist eindrucksvoll, was für wunderbare Ergebnisse globales Denken und Handeln hervorbringen kann. «Making Things» – «Dinge machen»: dieses simple Credo kennzeichnet die Selbstverständlichkeit, mit der Issey Miyake arbeitet. Er legte es der gleichnamigen Ausstellung zugrunde, die 1999 in der Fondation Cartier pour l'art contemporain in Paris eröffnet wurde und eine beeindruckende Bilanz seines bisherigen Schaffens zeigte.

Miyake ist ununterbrochen auf der Suche nach den Herausforderungen der menschlichen Bekleidung. Eine dieser Herausforderungen ist das Verhältnis zwischen Körper und Kleidung, das er auf vielfältige Weise neu interpretiert hat. Dabei erreicht Miyake mit seinen Entwürfen fast beiläufig eine unprätentiöse Schönheit, die aus einer anderen Welt zu stammen scheint, weil sie über Trends und Moden erhaben ist. Nun hat sich Miyake in dem selben Geist einer neuen Herausforderung gestellt: dem Herstellungsprozess von Bekleidung. Er begann die Arbeit an dieser Herausforderung gemeinsam mit Dai Fujiwara, einem der vielen Talente, die in den letzten Jahren aus dem Miyake Design Studio hervorgegangen sind. Gemeinsam haben sie den komplexen und vielschichtigen Herstellungsablauf von Kleidung völlig neu durchdacht – von der Generierung der Rohstoffe über die verwendeten Maschinen und die Auslieferung bis hin zur Anprobe durch den Benutzer. Das Ergebnis ist A-POC (A Piece Of Cloth). Nachdem im Jahr 2000 in Paris und Tokio jeweils ein A-POC-Schauraum eröffnet wurde, wird A-POC in diesem Buch und der dazu gehörigen Ausstellung erstmals außerhalb dieser beiden Städte vorgestellt.

Als Issey Miyake und Dai Fujiwara im Oktober 2000 das Vitra Design Museum Berlin besuchten, war unsere Berliner Dependance gerade einmal vier Monate jung. Miyake und Fujiwara erzählten begeistert von ihrem neuen Mode-Konzept und rollten dabei zahlreiche Stoffbahnen der A-POC-Kollektionen aus, die uns mit ihren Mustern und Durchbrüchen zuerst an Kelims erinnerten. Erst auf den zweiten Blick erkannten wir, daß sich in dieser Bahn eine komplette Kleidungsausstattung, inklusive Geldbörse, Tasche und Mütze verbarg, die man nur herausschneiden mußte! Die selbstverständliche Schönheit dieses Entwurfs faszinierte uns ebenso wie die konzeptionelle Stärke von A-POC. Denn in ihrer radikalen Grundlagenarbeit entspricht die Idee von A-POC einem Ideal von Design, das auch als Prämisse der Arbeit unseres Museums gilt: daß gelungenes Design aus der Kenntnis der eigenen Vorläufer seine Fundamente stets neu erfinden muß und erst daraus seine ästhetische Kraft bezieht. A-POC ist ein Beleg für die Wahrheit dieser These. Der Entscheidung, uns bei der geplanten Ausstellung ganz auf A-POC zu konzentrieren, folgte eine begeisternde und produktive Zusammenarbeit, deren Ergebnisse hier zu sehen sind und für die wir allen Beteiligten herzlich danken. Für das Vitra Design Museum Berlin ist die Ausstellung A-POC MAKING nicht nur die erste ausschließlich für unser Haus konzipierte Ausstellung, sondern auch eine Herausforderung für unsere zukünftige Arbeit.

A-POC beruht auf der Möglichkeit, mit neuartigen, computerprogrammierten Maschinen endlose Textilbahnen mit bislang unbekannten Eigenschaften herzustellen. So können in das Textil bestimmte Schnittmuster eingearbeitet werden, und ein raffiniertes System von Verbindungen und Durchbrüchen zwischen den beiden Seiten des Textilschlauchs ermöglicht, daß der Benutzer nahtlose Kleidungsstücke in unterschiedlichen Variationen herausschneiden kann.

Die Eigenschaften des Stoffs können durch den Computer punktuell bestimmt, manche der Stoffe gar an beliebigen Stellen geschnitten werden. Mit diesen Möglichkeiten löst A-POC sich von den Beschränkungen der klassischen Schneiderkunst, die durch die Eigenschaften von Stoff, Schnittmuster, Nähtechnik vorgegeben waren. Anstatt der strengen Matrix von Kette und Schuß, die in die Form des menschlichen Körpers genäht werden muß, entsteht ein nahtloses Kontinuum, das der menschlichen Haut so nahe wie niemals zuvor kommt.

A-POC läßt im Bereich der menschlichen Bekleidung eine Utopie Realität werden, die eines der zentralen Leitmotiv der Designgeschichte ist: ein Objekt aus einem Stück herzustellen. Man gebe einen Rohstoff in eine Maschine und entnehme am Ende das fertige Produkt! Dieser Traum ist weit mehr als reine Technikgläubigkeit. Seit den Anfängen der industriellen Revolution steht er für optimale Ressourcennutzung, Rationalisierung des Herstellungsprozesses und maschinengerechte Ästhetik. Durch Miyakes Werk zieht er sich als die Bestrebung, bei seinen Entwürfen von einem einzigen Stück Stoff auszugehen. Mit A-POC erreichen Miyake und Fujiwara dabei eine neue Dimension. Denn dank der Computertechnologie kann heute ein weiterer Rohstoff noch unmittelbarer in den Herstellungsprozess mit einfließen: menschliche Kreativität. Maschinen werden zu flexiblen Systemen, die bei der Verarbeitung des Rohstoffs direkt auf die Anweisungen des Gestalters reagieren. Ähnlich wie beim Computer-to-Plate-Druckverfahren oder bei Maschinen, die nach Computerzeichnungen umgehend das dreidimensionale Modell fräsen, wird aus einem komplizierten Ablauf ein kleiner Schritt, der jederzeit beeinflussbar ist. Auch auf der Benutzerseite schaffen Issey Miyake und Dai Fujiwara ungeahnte Gestaltungsspielräume, indem sie bei A-POC ein Element der Interaktivität vorsehen und den Benutzer sein eigenes Kleidungsstück herauslösen lassen. Das Ergebnis ist ein genial einfacher Prozess: Was zwei Designer angelegt haben und durch Maschinen als Rohling vervielfältigt wurde, kann der Benutzer am Ende seinen eigenen Wünschen und Bedürfnissen anpassen.

Aus der Grundidee von A-POC entwickelten Issey Miyake und Dai Fujiwara eine Vielzahl von Modellen und Variationen, die in diesem Buch vorgestellt werden. Ihre Ästhetik wird von allen Beteiligten zu gleichen Teilen geprägt: den Designern, der Technologie und dem Benutzer. Als Resultat einer echten Innovation hat diese Ästhetik eine innere Logik und ist weit mehr als à la mode. Vielmehr ist sie vergleichbar mit einer Ästhetik, wie sie sich im Möbeldesign in den zwanziger Jahren durchsetzte, als mit der Einführung von Stahlrohr völlig neue Produktions- und Gestaltungsvoraussetzungen gegeben waren. A-POC zeigt heute aufs Neue, daß die Einbindung neuer Technologien in die Formbildung etwas Klärendes haben kann, indem sie die Reduktion auf die Essenz des Objekts ermöglicht. Issey Miyake und Dai Fujiwara finden gestalterische Freiheit in der formalen Beschränkung und gewinnen zugleich völlig neue Möglichkeiten in der Interaktion zwischen Gestalter, Kleidung und Benutzer.

Wie anatomische Präparate breitet dieses Buch die A-POC-Objekte vor dem Auge des Betrachters aus. Mode wird zu Naturwissenschaft; Bekleidung wird seziert und von Beginn an neu buchstabiert. In diesem Sinne sind die Ausstellung A-POC MAKING und das vorliegende Buch als ein Blick in das Labor von Issey Miyake und Dai Fujiwara zu verstehen. Darin wird zwar nicht geklont oder gezaubert, doch arbeitet man an einem ganzheitlichen Bild des Menschen und seiner Bekleidung, das Epoche machen könnte. Es verbindet die individuellen Wünschen des Benutzers mit den Anforderungen eines ökonomischen Herstellungsprozesses; Computertechnologie mit Ressourcenschonung; eine einzigartige künstlerische Handschrift mit tragbarer Kleidung, die uns täglich begleiten kann. Und schließlich stellt es auch bei Mode wieder denjenigen in den Mittelpunkt, für den Kleidung gemacht wird. Denn wenn man sein eigenes Kleidungsstück aus dem A-POC-Textilschlauch herauslöst und sie überzieht, fühlt man sich selbst als Mode-Schöpfer. Oder so, wie zwei der ersten A-POC-Modelle heißen: als «King» oder «Queen».

Kleidung für die Zukunft Produkte aus Vorstellungskraft und Technologie / Issey Miyake

Nachdem ich im Jahr 2000 die Verantwortung für die Issey Miyake-Kollektionen an einen meiner Schüler abgegeben hatte, wartete ein Abenteuer auf mich. Die Reise, die wir unternahmen, führte uns zu einem Planeten, den wir A-POC nennen. Meine Begleiter und Partner bei dieser Reise sind Dai Fujiwara und mehrere andere junge Leute. Ich bin zuversichtlich, dass sie mit ihrer ganzen Kreativität und Unbefangenheit mit mir zusammen arbeiten werden, um Kleidung zu finden, die ihre Zeit und Lebensstil widerspiegelt – etwas, wonach ich immer suche.

In der zweiten Hälfte des neunzehnten Jahrhunderts kam es zur Industriellen Revolution, deren Haupterrungenschaften der Webstuhl und die Dampfmaschine waren. Dies hatte die Bildung einer neuen Mittelschicht zur Folge, vor allem nach der Französischen Revolution. Diese gesellschaftlichen und industriellen Umwälzungen veränderten die Geschichte der Bekleidung. Es entwickelte sich populäre Mode, die bis zu diesem Zeitpunkt ein Privileg der Aristokratie gewesen war. Dies sind vielleicht die Wurzeln der Haute Couture mit vielen neuen Ideen und eventuell auch die Vorläufer des Prêt-à-Porter. Schon immer gab es parallel zu den Veränderungen in der Welt unterschiedliche Modeerscheinungen.

Wieder einmal steht unsere Gesellschaft vor dramatischen Veränderungen in Wissenschaft und Technologie. Wird die Mode ihre alten Methoden beibehalten können? Ich wollte grundlegende Veränderungen in den Herstellungsprozessen von Kleidung einführen. Stellen Sie sich vor: Ein Faden läuft durch eine Maschine, die daraus mit Hilfe der neusten Computertechnologie Kleidungsstücke produziert und das normalerweise erforderliche Zuschneiden und Nähen des Stoffs überflüssig macht. Diese Idee entspringt meinem Wunsch, einen Beitrag zum Umweltschutz und zur Erhaltung der Rohstoffe zu leisten. Der Prozess spart nicht nur Rohstoffe und Arbeit, sondern auf diese Weise kann auch recycelt werden. Ich führte diese Idee zum ersten Mal unter dem Namen «Just Before» in meiner Frühjahr/Sommer-Kollektion 1998 ein. Verschiedene Kleiderformen wurden in einem fortlaufenden Schlauch angelegt, und die Vollendung nahm der Träger selbst vor. In der Frühjahr/Sommer-Kollektion 2000 wurde dieses Projekt A-POC genannt – es steht für A Piece Of Cloth und entwickelt sich seitdem weiter. Neuere Versionen waren «Woven» (eine einheitliche Formulierung von Textilien), «Mobile» (weiter gefasst), «Angel» (Kinderbekleidung) und «Framework» (die Variation bestimmter Rahmen). Wir sind noch immer dabei, aus A-POC Formeln für Industrieprodukte zu schaffen, und es gibt unzählige Möglichkeiten. Mit ein wenig Vorstellungskraft können wir sogar nicht nur Kleidung, sondern auch Roboter herstellen! Ich bin der Meinung, dass Technologie nur funktionieren kann, wenn wir genügend Kreativität besitzen, neugierig sind und unsere Mitmenschen lieben.

Das A-POC-Konzept entstand in Japan und wurde in Paris vorgestellt, einer Stadt, in der man Originalität zu schätzen weiß. A-POC wird nun erste Schritte in Berlin unternehmen, einem Ort, der für die Vereinigung von Ost und West steht. Mit jedem Besuch in Berlin bin ich stärker fasziniert von der Bereitschaft dieser Stadt, zur internationalen Gesellschaft zu gehören, von ihrer Fähigkeit, die unterschiedlichsten Kulturen zu schätzen und von der Dynamik des Wiederaufbaus. Es ist interessant, dass die Bauhaus-Tradition, die Integration von Kunst und Technologie, in Deutschland entstanden ist. Das Vitra Design Museum könnte als Erbe dieser Bewegung bezeichnet werden – untrennbar mit dem alltäglichen Leben verbunden. Im Besitz des Museums befindet sich eine riesige Sammlung von industriellem Möbeldesign. Es ist eines der ersten Museen, das sich auf Industriedesign konzentriert: die Integration von Kunst und Technologie. Insofern konnte das Museum unseren Wunsch sehr gut verstehen, Design für das 21. Jahrhundert in seiner intimsten Ausprägung zu entwickeln – in Form von menschlichen Kleidung.

Ich möchte an dieser Stelle dem Vitra Design Museum Berlin herzlich danken, dass es uns die Möglichkeit gegeben hat, unsere Arbeit auszustellen. Es würde mich hoch erfreuen, wenn die Einwohner Berlins an der Ausstellung A-POC MAKING Gefallen finden.

A-POC, A-POS, A-POM & A-POE / Dai Fujiwara

A-POC ist die Abkürzung für «A Piece of Cloth» und spielt mit dem Klang des englischen Wortes, das benutzt wird, um eine große Zeitspanne zu beschreiben: «Epoch». «A Piece of Cloth» ist ein sich ständig weiter entwickelndes Konzept, das den Epochenwechsel in eine Form bringen will. Wie mit einem unsichtbaren Faden sind wir alle mit den längst vergangenen Zeiten unseres Ursprungs und mit dem Wandel der Zeit verbunden, und dies ist auch bei A-POC der Fall. Der Produktionsprozess macht Fortschritte, wird aber niemals die Verbindung zum Wissen der vergangenen Zeiten verlieren.

A Piece of Cloth kann bis in alte Mythen zurückverfolgt werden. Man stelle sich folgendes Gemälde vor: Das eine Stück Stoff umhüllt die Schultern eines sinnlichen, himmlischen Mädchens; gezeichnet mit hellen, sanften Farben ist das ein A-POC. Das Kleidungsstück auf dem Gemälde tanzt, als würde es in der Luft schweben, zart und durchsichtig – ein Hinweis auf den technologischen Sachverstand. Das ist lange her. Ein Mensch muss dieses Gemälde geschaffen haben, und ich denke, A-POC muss schon damals existiert haben. A-POC hat schon immer Hoffnung, Mut und Träume in das Leben der Menschen gebracht.

In diesem Sinne nennen wir unseren Faden A-POS (A Piece of String). Noch ist unbekannt, wie viel Einfluss innovative Materialien haben, die dank jüngster nano- und biotechnologischer Entwicklungen hergestellt werden können, aber deren Ursprünge liegen in Materialien, welche zusammen mit Artefakten in alten Gräbern gefunden wurden. Ein unglaublich festes Material, aus dem mit einer revolutionären Spinntechnik ein dünner Faden hergestellt wurde, der dann wiederum weiter verarbeitet werden konnte. Der Faden konnte extrem leicht sein und schmelzen, wenn es direkter Sonneneinstrahlung ausgesetzt war.

Wenn ein bei Ausgrabungen entdeckter Faden einer bestimmten Ära chemisch analysiert wird, werden manchmal Moleküle von Seidenbast und Fibroin entdeckt: In diesem Fall können wir ihn als Seide identifizieren. Den Dokumenten kann man entnehmen, dass die Seidenfasern aus der Maotai- (Changsha Mawangadui-) Periode dünner waren als die heutigen Fasern. Seidenfasern können sehr fein sein, weil sie aus Polymeren hergestellt werden. Je länger die Faser ist, desto schneller kann sie gesponnen werden, so dass dadurch schließlich auch die Produktionskosten reduziert werden können.[1] Das Kleidungsstück in dem Gemälde scheint gleichsam zu schweben. Ich kann mir die Gesichter der alten Techniker vorstellen: Männer, die eine Art zu spinnen erfanden, die verhinderte, dass sich die dünnen Fäden miteinander verhedderten, und die Webstühle entwickelten, die fehlerfrei funktionierten; und sie beschäftigten sich mit der Frage, ob es besser wäre, das fertige Kleidungsstück gerollt oder gefaltet auszuliefern.

Im Hinblick auf die Anstrengungen und den Einfallsreichtum, mit dem wir bei Technologie und Produktionseffizienz Fortschritte machen, besteht in der Tat nur ein kleiner Unterschied zwischen den alten Zeiten und der Gegenwart. Die Geschichte der Seide enthält viele Innovationen. Es gibt zahlreiche Daten darüber – von der Seidenkultur in China bis zum Beweis der Mendelschen Gesetze mit Seidenraupen zu Beginn des 20. Jahrhunderts in Japan, die Entwicklung der Seidenraupen-Fütterung, die Technologie beim Spinnen der Fäden, genetische Kreuzungen und sogar das Klonen.[2] Die Vorstellungskraft hat A Piece of Cloth in der Geschichte vorangetrieben. Diese Kraft kann «A Power of Creation» genannt werden.

Wenn man all dies berücksichtigt, was kann die Menschheit dann noch erfinden, und wie sollen diese neuen Materialien genutzt werden? Vielleicht die Kreuzung einer Seidenraupe mit einer Spinne oder aus einer Reispflanze gewonnener Polyester? Würde man dies tun, würde sich der Begriff von «Natur» beziehungsweise die Vorstellung von den Dingen, die «natürlich» sind, zweifellos verändern. Es ist aufregend, sich zu überlegen, in welcher Weise solche Erfindungen A-POC beeinflussen würden.

Denken wir nun an die Maschinen. In der Welt von A-POC nennen wir unsere Maschine A-POM (A Piece of Machine). Bei der Herstellung von Kleidung ist das Grundprinzip von A-POM das Eins-und-Null-Prinzip der binären Sprache. Personen, die im Technik-Bereich arbeiten, würden bei dieser Beschreibung antworten: «Das ist ein Computer.» Bitte betrachten Sie das einfache Diagramm. Es sieht aus wie ein Schachbrett. Aber wenn das Diagramm an die Maschine übermittelt wird, bewegt sich der Faden auf und ab und webt oder strickt das Kleidungsstück. Weiß ist das Signal für «senken», und Schwarz ist das Signal für «Oberfläche»; die Maschine interpretiert das Diagramm und entnimmt daraus, ob sie ein Kleidungsstück weben soll, das in der Luft tanzen kann, oder ein T-Shirt herstellen soll. Die «Sprache» kann übermittelt werden: Wir können so programmieren, dass Schwarz «vorwärts» bedeutet und Weiß «rückwärts», und wir können sogar ein einfaches Spiel daraus machen. Wir nutzen die digitale Sprache zur Herstellung unserer Textilien. Zerlegt man ein Kleidungsstück von A-POC in seine digitalen Bestandteile, findet man zahlreiche Punkte. Wenn man diese Punkte als Gene in einem menschlichen Körper betrachtet, besteht jedes A-POC-Modell aus bis zu 200 Millionen «Genen». Wenn das digitale Muster des Kleidungsstücks einmal analysiert ist, kann man soviele wie nötig daraus «klonen».

Man benötigt eine mutige Belegschaft, um A-POC herzustellen, um Technologie und die Vorstellungskraft einzusetzen und fehlerfrei zu weben. Heutzutage kann man bei der Herstellung von A-POC die fortgeschrittenen Errungenschaften der digitalen Revolution nutzen.

Betrachtet man Kleidung aus Ausgrabungen, kann man sich vorstellen, dass die Techniker damals bereits die Grundlagen der Computertechnologie vorausgeahnt haben. In dieser Hinsicht besteht bei der Herstellung von Kleidungsstücken und der Verwendung von Fäden keinerlei Unterschied zwischen längst vergangenen Zeiten und den Informationen, die heutzutage die Köpfe der Techniker vernetzen. Auch wenn es in naher Zukunft künstliche Intelligenz geben sollte, würde das die Art und Weise, in der A-POC hergestellt wird, nicht grundlegend verändern. In der Tat wäre dies nur eine andere mögliche Spielart natürlicher Phänomene. Solange es Menschen gibt, die A-POS spinnen, A-POM bedienen und A-POC herstellen, brauchen wir wohl A-POE (A Person of Education), um die Produktion und die Geschäftsmethoden zu steuern und sich um die Belange der Umwelt zu kümmern.

Das Zwanzigste Jahrhundert war durch die Massenproduktion die «epische Epoche» hinsichtlich der Möglichkeit, Dinge in großer Menge und Verschiedenheit zu niedrigen Preisen zu produzieren. In der Prêt-à-Porter-Mode, der Entsprechung zur Massenproduktion in der Haute Couture, wechseln die Formen und Farben jede Saison. Dieser Trend steht im Gegensatz zum Design von Autos oder Haushaltsgeräten, die sich immer nur leicht verändern und immer dasselbe Produkt bleiben. Wenn hingegen die Prêt-à-Porter-Saison vorbei ist, muss in Windeseile etwas Neues geschaffen werden, und alles beginnt wieder von vorne. Es ist immer neu. Prêt-à-Porter war eine Innovation, weil sie die Produktionskosten senkte und gleichzeitig verschiedene Designs ermöglichte. In dieser Hinsicht könnte man das weltweit standardisierte System der computergestützten Produktion als Beginn einer Verwandlung zum Prêt-à-Porter-System betrachten.[3] Zur Reduzierung von Kosten wird Standardisierung verlangt, während die Vielfalt der Designs nötig ist, um der breiten Nachfrage der Kunden entsprechen zu können.

«Lasst uns anfangen», sagt Issey-san, wenn er ein Kleidungsstück in der Hand hält. Lasst uns beginnen, in Sekundenbruchteilen durch Raum und Zeit zu reisen und alle existierenden Wertvorstellungen hinter uns zu lassen; unsere Phantasie soll uns als Antrieb dienen.

[1] *«The Origin of Chinese Civilization»*, von Xia Nai;
veröffentlicht bei Nippon Hoso Kyokai, Tokio, 1984

[2] *«Theory of Silkworm Species», von Kametaro Sotoyama;*
veröffentlicht bei Maruyamasha Shosekibu, Tokio 1909

[3] *«The Machine That Changed the World»,*
hersausgegeben von Daniel Roos, Ph. D. James, P. Womack, Ph. D;
veröffentlicht bei RA Rawson Associates Scribner, New York, 1990.

A-POC 1997 – 2001

1997
Just Before
«Just Before» wurde im Rahmen der Issey Miyake Kollektion Frühling-Sommer 1998 am 15. Oktober in der Ecole des Beaux Arts, Paris vorgestellt. Eine Industriestrickmaschine wurde von einem Computer so programmiert, dass sie eine ganze Reihe an Strickkleidern und –blusen produzierte, die nahtlos ineinander übergingen. Jedes Kleidungsstück kann auf viele verschiedene Weisen herausgelöst werden. So hat jede Trägerin die Möglichkeit, entsprechend den eigenen Wünschen an der Kreation der eigen Kleidung mitzuwirken. Der Name «Just Before» deutet an, dass die so entstandenen Kleidungsstücke fertig zu sein scheinen, aber schließlich erst durch das Herauslösen wirklich vollendet werden. Dies war der Ausgangspunkt für die Entstehung von A-POC. Das Innovative an «Just Before» war die Entwicklung eines absolut neuartigen Herstellungsprozesses, der sich vom herkömmlichen Prêt-à-Porter unterscheidet, weil er den gesamten Prozess von den Garnen bis hin zum Kauf durch den Kunden einbezog. Das Kleidungsstück entsteht nicht durch die herkömmliche Methode des Schneidens und Nähen der Stoffe, es enthält seine Form vielmehr, indem verschiedenen Garne eine computerprogrammierte Maschine durchlaufen. Abschließend kann der Träger daran teilhaben, seine eigene Garderobe herzustellen.

1998
Die Entstehung von A-POC
Issey Miyake, der sich stets darum bemüht, dass der Herstellungsprozess von Kleidung den Anforderungen der Zeit gerecht wird, sah in dem neuen System ein unerschöpfliches Potential und begann damit, das A-POC-Projekt weiter zu entwickeln. «Tube Knit» wurde in der Issey Miyake Kollektion Herbst-Winter 1998 vorgestellt. Es ensteht wiederum aus verschiedenen, miteinander verbundenen Textilschläuchen. Dieser Herstellungsprozess eröffnet neue Möglichkeiten der Ressourcenschonung, da die Stoffabfälle durch den Verzicht auf unnötige Produktionsschritte erheblich verringert wurden.
King & Queen, Le Feu
Beide Modelle wurden in der Issey Miyake Kollektion Frühling-Sommer 1999 vorgestellt. Ein einziges Stück Stoff wurde auf den Boden der Eingangshalle der Ecole des Beaux Arts in Paris gelegt. Mitarbeiter des Designers lösten die einzelnen Teile heraus, und so verwandelte sich dieses Stück Stoff auf magische Weise in ein Kleid, Socken, einen Hut und eine Handtasche. Dies war der Beginn der Präsentation. Beim Finale schritt eine Prozession von Mannequins in den ursprünglichen, noch miteinander verbundenen Stoffbahnen durch den Raum.
Ausstellung «ISSEY MIYAKE MAKING THINGS»
in der Fondation Cartier pour l'art contemporain, Paris
Diese Ausstellung, die Issey Miyakes Schaffen der letzten 10 Jahre als Schwerpunkt hatte, wurde vom 1. Oktober 1998 bis 29. Februar 1999 in der Fondation Cartier für zeitgenössische Kunst in Paris gezeigt. Das A-POC-Projekt zog als eine Idee für die Herstellung von Kleidung für die Zukunft besondere Aufmerksamkeit auf sich.

1999
Alien, Eskimo
Beide Modelle waren Bestandteil der Issey Miyake Kollektion Herbst-Winter 1999, die am 10. März in La Grande Halle de la Villette, Salle Charlie Parker, Paris, stattfand. «Alien» besteht aus doppelten Stofflagen in luftig gestrickten Maschen, die zahlreiche Variationen der Designs ermöglichen. «Eskimo» mit seinen geometrischen Mustern und eingearbeiteten Leisten ist ein dreideimensionales Kleidungsstück.
Vorstellung von A-POC
Das Label A-POC wurde erstmals am 29. März im Jingumae Studio in Tokio vorgestellt. Die erste A-POC-Kollektion umfaßte gleich die Modelle für Frühling-Sommer sowie für Herbst-Winter 1999.
Jeux de Tissu (Stoffspiele) von Yayoi Kusama
Diese Performance fand am 9. April in der französischen Botschaft in statt. Die Avantgarde-Künstlerin Yayoi Kusama präsentierte die Kunstperformance «Jeux de Tissu» unter Verwendung von «King» und «Queen» als Leinwand. Kusama besprühte die weißen Modelle mit fluoreszierenden Farbpunkten, die im Dunkeln leuchteten, und nannte sie «Dots Obsession».
A-POC Kollektion Frühjahr-Sommer 2000
Sie wurde in der Galerie Ghislaine Hussenot in Paris am 5. Oktober 2000 vorgestellt. Darunter waren: «Millenium Pillow» (das Kleidungsstücke, Accessoires und ein Kissen enthält), «Baguette» (das an jeder beliebigen Stelle beschnitten werden kann), «Pain de mie» (aus einfach gewebten Stoffen), «Feuille» (mit Blumenmuster) und «Spider» (ein extrem elastisches Modell).
Ausstellung ISSEY MIYAKE MAKING THINGS in der
ACE Gallery, New York
Die Ausstellung wurde vom 11. November 1999 bis zum 29. Februar 2000 in New York gezeigt. Es lag bereits ein größerer Schwerpunkt auf den A-POC-Ausstellungsstücken.

2000

Eröffnung des ersten A-POC Schauraums in Aoyama/Tokio
Die Hauptsitz von A-POC wurde am 17. Februar in Aoyama/Tokio eröffnet. Der 234 Quadratmeter große Raum umfaßt nicht nur eine Verkaufsfläche, sondern auch einen Arbeitsbereich für Designexperimente und ein Studio, das man auf Grund seiner gläsernen Trennwände auch von außen einsehen kann. Indem das Studio mit dem Verkaufsbereich zu einem großen Raum verbunden ist, wird das Konzept, dass der Träger der Kleidung in den kreativen Herstellungsprozess eingebunden wird, auch architektonisch veranschaulicht.
Space Design: Tokujin Yoshioka
Adresse: 3-17-14 Minami-Aoyama, Minato-Ku, Tokio.

Teilnahme an der Ausstellung Utsu in Stockholm
Die Ausstellung Utsu fand vom 15. Mai bis zum 18. August im Museum für Fernöstliche Kunst in Stockholm, Schweden statt. Das Motto dieser Ausstellung lautete: «Das Herz der japanischen Kunst liegt in der Wahrnehmung des Unsichtbaren». Gezeigt wurden Werke von vier Künstlern, die die zeitgenössische japanische Kultur repräsentierten. Von Issey Miyake waren A-POC «King» und «Queen» in den Farben der Flaggen beider Länder zu sehen.

Vorstellung der A-POC Herbst-Winter Kollektion 2000 in Paris
Die Kollektion wurde am 5. Juni im Fondation Cartier für zeitgenössische Kunst in Paris gezeigt. Unter den vorgestellten Stücken befand sich «Dots Obsession» von Yayoi Kusama, «Angel» (für Kinder), «Mobile» (ein variables Möbel- und Bekleidungsobjekt), «Fringe», «Caravan» und «Pollen».

Vorstellung der A-POC Herbst-Winter 2000 Kollektion in Tokio
Diese Kollektion wurde im A-POC Schauraum in Tokio vom 7. – 9. Juni 2000 vorgestellt.

Eröffnung des A-POC Schauraums in Paris
Der zweite A-POC Schauraum wurde am 7. September 2000 in Paris eröffnet. Er wurde von Ronan und Erwan Bouroullec gestaltet. Die Ausstellungsräume können durch bewegliche Trennwände beständig variiert werden; Schneidetische ermöglichen die umgehende Anpassung der A-POC Modelle an die Kundenwünsche.

Verleihung des japanischen Design Grand Prize
Am 13. Oktober 2000 erhält A-POC den Grand Prize der japanischen Gesellschaft für Industriedesign. Die Jury begründete ihre Entscheidung mit den zwei revolutionären Aspekte von A-POC. Der erste Aspekt bezieht sich darauf, daß Mode erstmals unter industriellen Gesichtspunkten erdacht und gestaltet wurde. Der zweite bezieht sich auf die innovative Produktionsweise, die es ermöglicht, zwei sich scheinbar widersprechende Ideen, die der individuellen Anpassung und die der Massenproduktion, gleichermaßen zu verwirklichen.

Vorstellung der Kollektion Frühling-Sommer 2001 im Schauraum der Issey Miyake Inc., Tokyo

2001

A-POC Kollektion Frühling-Sommer 2001 in Paris
Die Präsentation fand am 8. Februar 2001 in den Schauräumen von Issey Miyake Paris statt. Unter den gezeigten Stücken waren: sechs Kleider aus der Serie «One Piece», von denen jedes aus einem einzigen Faden und im selben Muster hergestellt ist, «Baguette» mit vier Variationen, nach denen man ein Hemd herauslösen kann und zahlreiche andere Modelle.

Acknowledgements

The exhibition A-POC MAKING is shown at
Vitra Design Museum Berlin June 1 – July 1, 2001

This project could not have been accomplished without the participation of many indidviduals.

Special thanks are due to Irving Penn for the cover photograph and to Kartell for the exhibition chairs.

We would like to express our heartfelt thanks to Issey Miyake and Dai Fujiwara for their inspiration and confidence in our common project.

SHARP

Picture Credits

Cover photograph: copyright © 1999 Irving Penn

10, 11: Pascal Roulin
12: Yasuaki Yoshinaga
13–16: Pascal Roulin
17: Yasuaki Yoshinaga
18-23: Pascal Roulin
24-27: Yasuaki Yoshinaga
28, 29: Pascal Roulin
30: Yasuaki Yoshinaga
32: Pascal Roulin
33-35: Yasuaki Yoshinaga
37-41: Pascal Roulin
42–47: Yasuaki Yoshinaga
48-56: Pascal Roulin
57-59: Yasuaki Yoshinaga
77: Naohiro Tsutsuguchi (Geijutsu Shincho)
79: Osamu Kobayashi (Asahi Shimbun News Paper)
82: Yasuaki Yoshinaga
85, top: Françoise Huguier
85, bottom right: Yasuaki Yoshinaga
85, bottom left: Françoise Huguier
86, 87: Mitsumasa Fujitsuka
88, top: Ling Fei
88, bottom left and right: Yasuaki Yoshinaga
90, top: Nacàsa & Partners, Inc.
90, bottom: S. Anzai
93: Morgane Le Galli
94, 95: Françoise Huguier
97: Friedemann Hauss
99, 100: Marcus Tomlinson/i-D magazine
112: Thorsten Romanus

Imprint

A-POC MAKING: ISSEY MIYAKE & DAI FUJIWARA
is a co-production of Vitra Design Museum Berlin
with Miyake Design Studio

Catalogue

Editors
Mateo Kries, Alexander von Vegesack

Concept
Mateo Kries, Thorsten Romanus

Visual Director
Midori Kitamura

Authors
Issey Miyake, Dai Fujiwara, Mateo Kries

Design
Büro für Gestaltung, Thorsten Romanus

Graphic Support
Bellinda Behnke

Translations
Jutta Küster, Berlin

Co-ordination of Production
Elke Henecka

Lithography and Printing
GZD Grafisches Zentrum Drucktechnik,
Ditzingen-Heimerdingen

Special thanks to Nobuko Kojima, pH studio Inc.,
Miyake Design Studio, Issey Miyake Inc.,
Issey Miyake Europe S.A., Issey Miyake USA Corp.,
Issey Miyake London Ltd., Roy Genty, Omori Masako,
and the A-POC team (Dai Fujiwara, Daisaku Mizuuchi,
Masami Umezawa, Masaru Takahashi) for their
contribution to the catalogue and the exhibition.

Exhibition

Exhibition Director
Issey Miyake

Concept
Issey Miyake, Dai Fujiwara

Space Design
Tokujin Yoshioka

Visual Director
Midori Kitamura

Co-ordination
Mateo Kries

Organisation
Omori Masako, Mariko Onda, Marie Chalmel,
Valérie Lebérichel, Mateo Kries, Britt Angelis

Animations
Pascal Roulin

Technical Realisation
Vitra Design Museum

Technical Staff
Thomas Schweikert, Thierry Hodel,
Bernd Nickel, Thomas Moll

Public Relations
Britt Angelis, Gianoli PR, Valérie Lebérichel

Visitors Service
Judith Flörke, Ariane Seeger

Vitra Design Museum always does its utmost to respect the rights of third parties. Should we have overlooked this in individual cases then such oversights will be rectified as soon as possible.

© 2001 Vitra Design Museum and authors
© 2001 Issey Miyake Inc.
© 2001 Miyake Design Studio
Cover photograph: copyright © 1999 by Irving Penn

Distribution:
Vitra Design Museum GmbH
Weil am Rhein/Germany
shop@design-museum.de

ISBN 3-931936-26-0